The Romance OF Flowers

ISBN: 978-1-989872-15-4

First Published in Canada, 2025.
Published by Southernwood Technologies Inc. 2025.

Visit cheryllawson.net for more information about the author.

Dedicated to

The Pollinators

CONTENTS

The Seasons

Journey through the seasons

– **Winter, Spring, Summer and Autumn** –

in poems that attempt to capture the essence and emotion of

each studied moment.

Winter Slumber

Winter brings rest.
The job is done.
Frost before the snow,
snow before the sleep.
A well earned respite
from the task of survival.
Parchment petals
hold summer's last secrets:
Bee and wasp,
butterfly and ant
communed to spread
The Love.
Cast the joy wide,
shared the garden splendour
with one last wander.

Rose Bud

Bloom bust, cancelled by the chill.
Caught in suspended animation,
her job unfinished.

Rose Bud, they called her.
Rose bud she stayed;
cloaked in cold,
waiting for her moment that never came.

Would she see the sun again?
Would it dance on her bright red lips?
Frosted tips adorned her.
The coolness, a silver shiver.

Slowly, reds fade.
Green turns grey.
She softens and hardens all together,
Insides sagging against a crisp, frozen shell.

❋

Camelia

Pastel flattery, delicate skin.
Artful and sophisticated,
heady and mysterious.
This girl has it all, and then some.

But out in the cold,
fragile beauty doesn't keep up.
Too much summer.
Too much sun.

Frosted edges,
brown, brittle, breakable.
Camelia's heart's not in it anymore.
Her winter comes, the pinks become beige.

The world forgets her,
passes by her,
doesn't see her.
She fades to grey, mysterious no more.

Defrosting March turns
Soggy April.
Winter melts away,
giving it up to the drip, drip, drip of
Spring's opening chords.

May bursts in,
bright and new.
Born of the long, dark time before.
After the drip; ahead of the dry.
Her time is now, she knows the score.

Bird-song eschews the riot of Spring.
Petals and wings unfurl.
Leaves and paws uncurl.
Colour swirls against a vivid sky.
To be renewed is to rejoice.

Spring Enters, Soft & Sleepy

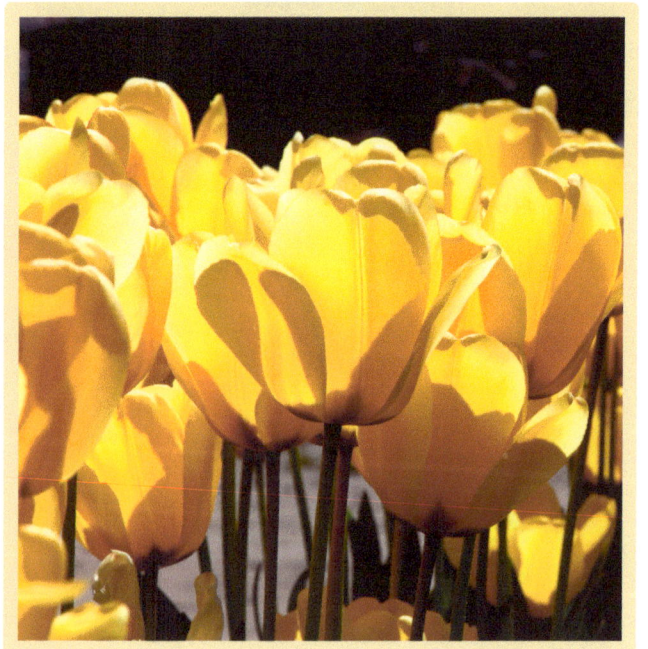

A Contest of Colour

"I'm Gorgeous!" they yell,
their colours, curves and flirt at full fire.
Unusual, outrageous, simultaneously
joyful at the arrival
of their favourite time of year.

SPRING!
Time to shine. Time to show off
the best, the brightest, the fascinating.
A fleeting dance and jostle for control
The megawatt stunners in the lead:
Tulip, Rose and Apple Blossom.

But in comes Lily, all smiles,
the gentle and shy Sage,
the slow to shine Hyacinth,
And Daisy, country girl and simple beauty.

"She's gorgeous!" they yell.

On the Wings of Summer

Silent, the drift and swoop.
Down and touch a bloom,
the glowing center:
A beacon.
Unfurl proboscis.
Drink in
Sweet nectar.

Life.
A brief moment
that lasts forever
continued in next year's blossoms,
when I'll be gone.
A promise of more to come,
carried on the wings
of Summer.

Exotic

Tropical heat hangs heavy.
A thunderstorm brews at sea.
Paradise has suspended time,
there are no clocks here.
No reminders to churn up
winter woes and snow slush.
The scented air,
rich with floral promise
clings to dampness that grows sultry
in the midday simmer.

Summer Sizzle

The heat bakes in
the fading hues.
Flowers wilt, awaiting rain.

Tougher blooms
proudly flaunt their summer sizzle,
Their pizzazz;
razzmatazz.
Displays of
insane defiance.

A cool breeze promises
the thirst will end.
The garden sings the cicada song.
A distant rumble rolls,
A cloud swells.
Fat drop farewells
to the sun.

Autumn Ushers In

Heavy hangs the bloom,
Sunflower and mums.
Another season is done.
The corn is grown,
A maze is drawn.
Soon pumpkin ghouls
the world will adorn.

October is close,
you can tell from the chill.
The dark is coming,
One last summer thrill.

To the field we go,
our harvest awaits.
One last hurrah is coming,
A night of fun and wraiths.

Once Upon A Garden

Imagination comes alive in a garden.

Yards transform into sanctuaries.

Purpose begets peace.

Peace invites Happiness.

Look Up

Just as in a garden cultivated to erupt into
joyous colour in Spring, the life we lead can be
a trove of dormant potential. There is joy in the
simple pleasures we tease out of the everyday.

Look Up!

Look Down!

Look Around,

And revel in the world's creativity

found in the everyday.

Life . . .

. . . like rain, can be heavy some days.

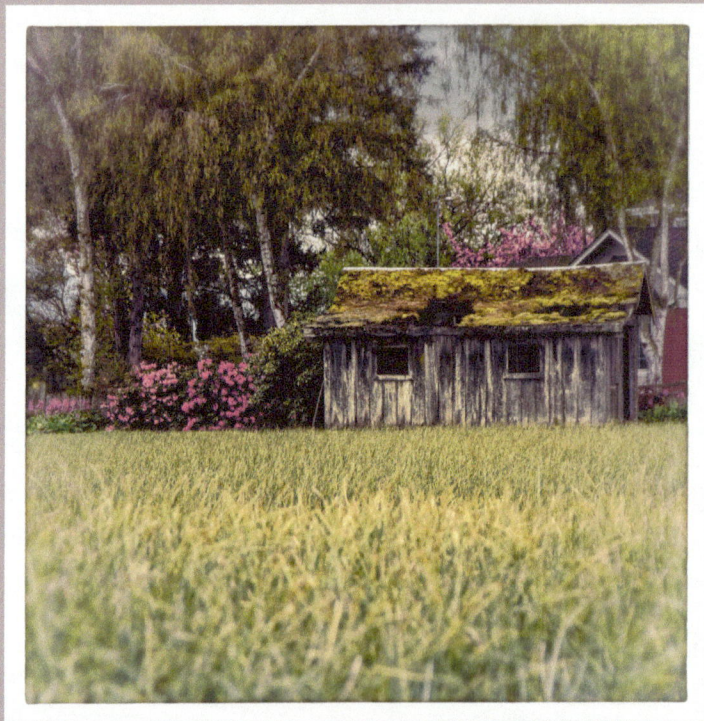

The Art of Neglect

Not every edge demands perfection. Not every lawn needs to be mowed.
There is an art to neglect, because in the act, nature is revealed.
It takes over, removes the stricture, smoothes the edges, makes way for
softening of the once-precise.

A garden can be more than order. It can be life. It can be lived-in, home to
thriving wonder.

A world in the weeds exists that confounds the perfectionist, astounds the
naturalist, delights the artist.

Rot isn't death. It is life.
Fade isn't ugly, it is a less-demanding state of being.
Overgrown is understated splendour.

Time fades us, blunts our minds.

The clarity disappears before the horizon these days.

Don't forget! Remember your Life!

It is all too much.

Where once there was definition,

there is now only jagged confusion, sadness, worry, and loss.

"Mum, it's me."

A stranger calls me mother. I feel bad for her. I feel bad for me.

We are both lost as the light fades and the edges blur.

I try! Oh, how I try!

Tomorrow might be better.

"Let's walk in the garden."

Familiarity rings. A happy glimmer.

Yes. The garden.

It knows me. And I know it.

In Memory of . . . .

Fruits of Love

Life starts with a seed tucked away inside a promise.

Beautiful, succulent, juicy bearer of possibility.

Glowy, showy, sexy and created for temptation.

Cultivated to bursting ripeness.

◉ ◉ ◉

Where there is whimsy,
there is fun, there is light,
there is Life.

Making Magic

Pond of Plenty

Nature strives to outperform,
Survival is teeming ecology.
It's in the numbers, volume, size, variety.
Creativity in form, flexing, changing, adapting.

Nature's abundance is wondrous.
Seek to copy its persistence; its vigour.
To know abundance, is to have joy.
To be joyful is life beyond surviving.

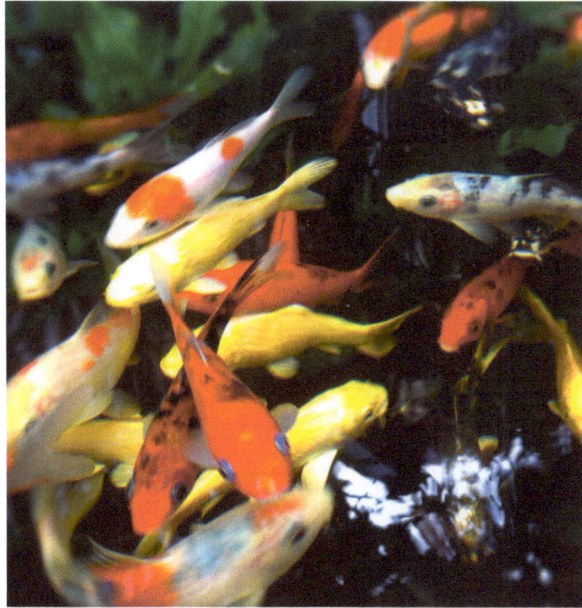

No Defined Path

Wildly beautiful lives
can have messy edges.
But they are filled with overlaps of
colour, vibrancy, and light.

Make space for imagination

and you'll never have a grey sky again.

❋

Rough-hewn Love

When we love completely, the world blossoms for us.

So, when you love:

Be warm in the shade,

be cool in the sun.

Be the wet in the dry,

be the island in a stream.

Shelter a fragile heart

and it will bloom even in hard ground.

Lavender Life

Purple courage when life gets hard.

A bracing scent to restore.

Garden of happiness, where bees and birds guard

this Lavender Life. All nature.

I pause gently,

sit quietly,

feel evenly,

And breathe out.

Every petal holds a secret.

Every secret is yours to discover.

Every discovery is a gift.

Every gift, a flower.

Let Nature Rule ...

Her wisdom is persistent.
Her intuition, paramount.
She knows more
than we could fathom in a lifetime.
She is Mother Earth.

Pollinator Power

Bees.

Flies.

Moths.

Wasps.

Beetles.

Butterflies.

Dragonflies.

Ants.

Spiders.

Let them be.

They have

important work.

Meadow Magic

No lawn, just flowers.

We built a space to linger,
You and I.
Here, we dance through daisies,
Lounge in the lavender,
Commune with the coneflowers,
and soak in rays with sunflowers.

And here I linger,
even when you are gone.
Here we are together
in this meadow we built.

Foxglove on a roadside – bees don't care.
A flower is a flower,
though if it's wild, its all the sweeter.
Lupine Love.
Daisy Divine.
Wildflower Hearts beat faster.

Wildflower Wow

Thank You

For journeying with me
through this garden of love.
Thanks for staying a while
and exploring this trove.
Goodbye from the blooms and pollinator friends.
I hope you leave with a smile,
Our trip has come to its end.

Photography and illustration by
Cheryl Bezuidenhout
Poetry and prose by
Cheryl Bezuidenhout

This book is testament to the beauty of the floral kingdom. We are truly fortunate to be able to appreciate the glorious colours, fragrances, textures and contrasts flowers present. With so much variety, both in cultivated species, as well as wildflowers, there is no shortage of floral joy to savour, but we must protect the pollinators who bring us this joy. Without them, the world's colours will be diminished, our gardens will vanish, the concrete and glass wins. So, plant more wildflowers, do a little less pruning, mowing and raking, save some messy spaces all year-round for the smallest inhabitants to thrive.

I do hope you've enjoyed this book. It is presented as journeys to captivate and provoke thought and mindfulness, reverence and love, care and stewardship.

Thank you for reading.

Cheryl.